Forever Inspired COLORING BOOK

CONFIDENT, STRONG, BEAUTIFUL, FUN

Copyright 2019 © by Racehorse for Young Readers

All rights reserved. No part of this book may be reproduced in any manner without the express written consent of the publisher, except in the case of brief excerpts in critical reviews or articles. All inquiries should be addressed to Racehorse Publishing, 307 West 36th Street, 11th Floor, New York, NY 10018.

Racehorse for Young Readers books may be purchased in bulk at special discounts for sales promotion, corporate gifts, fund-raising, or educational purposes. Special editions can also be created to specifications. For details, contact the Special Sales Department, Skyhorse Publishing, 307 West 36th Street, 11th Floor, New York, NY 10018 or info@skyhorsepublishing.com.

Racehorse for Young Readers™ is a pending trademark of Skyhorse Publishing, Inc.®, a Delaware corporation.

Visit our website at www.skyhorsepublishing.com.

10 9 8 7 6 5 4 3 2 1

Cover and interior artwork by John Kurtz

Print ISBN: 978-1-63158-464-0

Printed in China

Forever Inspired COLORING BOOK

CONFIDENT, STRONG, BEAUTIFUL, FUN

JOHN KURTZ

FOR YOUNG READERS

I Am
Adventurous

I Am
Artistic
1
2
3
4
5

I Am
A Star

I Am
Athletic

I Am
Beautiful

1
I Am
Brave

I Am
Careful

I Am
Caring

I Am
Clever

I Am
Colorful

I Am
Confident

I Am
Crafty

I Am
Creative

I Am Curious

I Am Fancy

JOKES
I Am
Funny

I Am
Giving

I Am
Growing

I Am Happy

I Am Healthy

I Am Helpful

I Am
Imaginative

I Am
Inventive

I Am
Loving

I Am
Mighty

I Am Musical

I Am
Nimble

I Am Noble

I Am
Patient

I Am Peaceful

I Am Playful

HELLO!
PLEASE
THANK YOU
YOU'RE WELCOME
I Am
Polite

I Am Positive
HAPPY

I Am
Powerful

I Am
Protective

I Am Reliable

I Am
Self-Reliant

I Am
Strong

I Am
Sweet

I Am
Talented

I Am
Thankful

I Am
Thoughtful

I Am Unique
UNIQUE

I Am
Unstoppable

Color Bars

Use these bars to test your coloring medium and palette. Don't be afraid to try unique color combinations!

Color Bars

Use these bars to test your coloring medium and palette. Don't be afraid to try unique color combinations!

Color Bars

Use these bars to test your coloring medium and palette. Don't be afraid to try unique color combinations!

Color Bars

Use these bars to test your coloring medium and palette. Don't be afraid to try unique color combinations!